ROBERTO CLEMENTE
AND THE WORLD SERIES UPSET

ROBERTO CLEMENTE

AND THE
WORLD SERIES UPSET

by Julian May

Published by Crestwood House, Inc., Mankato, Minnesota 56001. Published simultaneously in Canada by J. M. Dent and Sons, Ltd. Library of Congress Catalog Card Number: 73-80421. International Standard Book Number: 0-913940-01-1. Text copyright © 1973 by Julian May Dikty. Illustrations copyright © 1973 by Crestwood House, Inc. All rights reserved. No part of this book may be reproduced in any form without written permission from the publisher, except for brief passages included in a review. Printed in the United States of America.

Designed by William Dichtl

Crestwood House, Inc., Mankato, Minn. 56001

ROBERTO CLEMENTE
AND THE WORLD SERIES UPSET

A hot, tropical wind blew. Palm trees swayed around the baseball field.

All the boys but one had gone home to supper. This little fellow, hardly six years old, still played on. He threw the ball high into the air, then pretended to field it.

When he finally went home, his mother scolded him. "Your supper is cold! You and your baseball! Would you rather play ball than eat?"

And little Roberto Clemente smiled and said: "Yes."

He was born in 1934, on the beautiful island of Puerto Rico. It is a tropical land, without a cold winter. An airplane must fly 1,000 miles to travel from Miami to Puerto Rico's capital, San Juan.

The people of the island mingled the blood of many races in their veins—black, white, and Indian. Their skins were every color from pale tan to deep black. But every person was full of dignity and self-respect. People were judged by their work, not color.

The Clemente family lived in Carolina, a town not far from San Juan.

The flags of Puerto Rico and the United States fly side by side on the day in 1952 when the island became a commonwealth. The people of Puerto Rico are citizens of the United States, but they have their own independent government.

Children of Puerto Rico explore El Morro, an ancient fort guarding the harbor of San Juan.

A young sugar worker nibbles on a sweet piece of sugar cane.

When Roberto was born, Puerto Rico was a colony of the United States. Much of the land was owned by rich sugar companies. The people were very poor. Some of them did not have enough to eat.

The Clemente family was luckier than most. Mr. Clemente was a foreman on a sugar plantation. His wife helped him to run a grocery store. All the Clemente children had jobs to help out. Little Roberto delivered milk. He was paid 30 cents a month.

In the 1940's, great changes came to Puerto Rico. The big plantations were broken up. The people elected their own governor. Life began to improve for the poor.

In 1952, Puerto Rico became a commonwealth. Its people were citizens of the United States. But they governed themselves at last.

Truckloads of sugar cane rolled to the mills in 1949 as part of Operation Bootstrap. This was Puerto Rico's great self-help operation, which helped to relieve poverty.

In high school, Roberto was an outstanding baseball player. He was a track star, too. The coach wanted him to try out for the 1952 Olympic Team. He surely would have made it—but baseball got in the way.

One day, when Roberto was playing ball, he was seen by Pedro Zorilla. Zorilla owned the Santurce Crabbers, a professional baseball team in the Puerto Rican Winter League.

Zorilla watched Roberto attack the ball. The boy sprayed the field with line drives. He hit so hard that he leaped off the ground with both feet.

"This boy plays like a man," Zorilla thought. "I must have him for my team."

The five-team Puerto Rican league featured many stars from the mainland. In 1954, these fans welcomed Willie Mays by shooting off Roman candles.

Mr. and Mrs. Clemente were not too happy when Zorilla talked to them. They wanted Roberto to be an engineer—not a baseball player. But the boy begged them to let him play. Finally it was agreed. He would receive a salary of $60 a month, a $500 bonus—and a new fielder's glove.

The next season, the Dodgers had a clinic in San Juan. Roberto was one of 72 boys who tried out. Scout Alex Campanis asked Roberto to throw from the outfield. A ball came sizzling in, arrow-straight. Campanis had all the boys run. Roberto made the dash in 6.4 seconds. None of the others were near him.

Campanis asked Roberto to hit. The scout said a prayer: "Just let him be able to hold a bat!"

Roberto smacked the ball all over the field— right, left, and center. Campanis rejoiced. He could not sign Roberto until he graduated. But when that day came, the Dodgers were waiting.

He signed a contract for $10,000. Then he found himself on an airplane heading for Montreal, Canada. Why wasn't he going to Brooklyn?

They told him the Dodgers' roster was already full of heavy talent. Their fielding spots were held by men such as Jackie Robinson, Pee Wee Reese, Gil Hodges, Duke Snider, and Carl Furillo. There was no room for a kid—not even one as good as Roberto Clemente.

So they were putting him on Montreal's AAA farm team rather than having him ride the bench.

The star-studded 1954 Brooklyn Dodgers. *Seated left to right:* George Shuba; Tom LaSorda; Pee Wee Reese; Ted Lyons; Billy Herman; Manager Walter Alston; Jake Pitler; Billy Loes; Russ Meyer; Johnny Podres; Clem Labine. *Second row:* Lee Scott, traveling secretary; Harold Wendler, trainer; Pete Wojey; Duke Snider; Carl Furillo; Preacher Roe; Gil Hodges; Jackie Robinson; Al Walker; Don Newcombe; Walt Moryn; Wally Signer, batting practice pitcher; John Griffin, clubhouse custodian. *Third row:* Roy Campanella; Junior Gilliam; Jim Hughes; Don Zimmer; Carl Erskine; Sandy Amoros; Erv Palica; Don Hoak; Billy Cox; Bob Darnell.

But a funny thing happened during that 1954 season. Roberto played in only 87 games. It seemed that whenever he got hot, Manager Max Macon yanked him out.

"Why can't I play?" he asked sadly.

Macon replied: "You just sit tight, kid. It's for your own good."

But Roberto did not understand at all. He wanted to go home. Al Campanis tried to cheer him up. "They are *hiding* you, kid," he explained. "You're so good that if we're not careful, another team might draft you away from us!"

There was a new bonus rule that year. Any kid signed for more than $4,000 and not placed on the big-league roster right away could be drafted by another ball club.

Roberto Clemente in Montreal Royals uniform.

Old Forbes Field, former home of the Pittsburgh Pirates, is shown jammed with fans in 1960. When Roberto Clemente began to play there, in 1955, the crowds were very small because the team was a loser. In July, 1970, the Pirates moved to a brand-new ball park, Three Rivers Stadium.

Roberto's pride would not allow him to play poorly. During one game, he was spotted by Clyde Sukeforth, a scout for the Pittsburgh Pirates.

Sukeforth watched the boy from Puerto Rico play. He grinned at Max Macon and got only a scowl in return.

"Pittsburgh will end up in the cellar, Max. And the first thing we're gonna do after that is draft this boy. Take good care of him for us!"

The Dodgers won the pennant by 13 games. The Pirates were last—for the third time running. Having the first draft choice, they took Roberto for a mere $4,000.

When Roberto got the news he was amazed. "But where *is* Pittsburgh?" he asked.

"You'll find out soon enough," growled Max Macon.

18

After the season, Roberto went home to Puerto Rico. He played for Santurce in the Winter League. But the winter of 1954-55 proved to be a sad one. One of his brothers died. And Roberto himself was in an auto accident. It left him with a very sore back.

More unhappiness waited for him in spring. The Pirates' training camp was in Florida. He found out that he could not eat at the same restaurants as the white players. He could not even stay at the same motels. It was all very different from Montreal, where nobody had paid much attention to his color.

Roberto was proud and very sensitive. He would show these *Yanquis,* who made fun of his black skin and his Spanish language! He would show them how to play ball!

The 1955 Pirates lineup *(left to right):* Manager Bobby Bragan; Roberto Clemente, right field; Dick Groat, shortstop; Dale Long, first base; Frank Thomas, left field; Gene Freese, third base; Toby Atwell, catcher; Bobby Del Greco, center field; Johnny O'Brien, second base; Dick Hall, pitcher.

Manager Fred Haney saved Roberto for the home-town opener. A large crowd—very rare in those days—came to see the Pirates play the Dodgers.

Roberto was third in the lineup. He gripped the bat and narrowed his eyes to slits. Pitcher Johnny Podres let go the ball.

He lashed out. He connected for an infield single. Then teammate Frank Thomas hit a triple and Roberto got his first big-league run in his first big-league game.

The happy fans screamed. Things were going to be different from now on!

But it was a vain hope. The Pirates lost the game, 10-3. They dropped the other half of the double-header, 3-2. Roberto managed a single and a double in four times at bat.

Then the Pirates went to New York. Roberto got a home run. But the team lost, 12-3. It was not until their ninth game, against the Phillies, that they finally won. Roberto helped with a single and a double that brought two men home. He was batting .360.

Roberto crosses the plate as umpire Stan Landes watches.

Three baseball greats played together in the 1961 All-Star Game: Roberto Clemente, Willie Mays, and Henry Aaron.

But a baseball team is more than one rookie. Manager Haney had brought in younger players. But he could not inspire the team to win. The Pirates plunged to the cellar as usual and stayed there.

Even Roberto's fine start lost some steam. Rival pitchers discovered that he would swing at almost anything. They sent him a lot of bad balls.

At season's end, he had an average of .255. But already there was a flash of the superstar who was to come. A TV announcer wanted to praise him.

"You remind me of another young man who could hit, throw, and run—a fellow named Willie Mays!"

But Roberto only said proudly: "Nevertheless, I play like Roberto Clemente!"

In 1956 the Pirates got a new manager. Bobby Bragan tried hard to turn the team around. For awhile in June, the Pirates were in first place.

Roberto Clemente, with a batting average of .357 at that time, was third leading hitter in the league. But he still couldn't resist swinging at every baseball that flew past his bat.

Bragan worked hard to tame his Latin fireball and to shape the rest of the club into a winning machine. But it was not yet the time. After a great start, the Pirates sagged. They finished seventh. But everybody agreed they were much improved.

Playing against Brooklyn on September 29, 1956, Roberto made a brilliant diving catch of a ball hit by Pee Wee Reese.

Roberto shows a young fan, Junior James, where he likes to connect with the ball.

For a brief time in 1956, the Pirates were in first place and smiles filled the locker room. Sharing in horseplay are *(left to right):* Roberto Clemente, Dale Long, Ron Kline, Frank Thomas.

Roberto's final average that year was a healthy .311. Off the field, things did not go so well. He was lonely in Pittsburgh. There were very few Spanish-speaking people. Only the kids, asking for autographs, seemed friendly.

Some ball players try to avoid the fans. But not Roberto. He signed each autograph with a smile.

Back home in Puerto Rico, he played in the Winter League again, even though he was very tired. The result was new injury to his already sore back.

He was in great pain and had to wear a brace. His parents tried to make him quit baseball and go back to school.

"Let me play one more year," he said. "Then, if it still hurts, I'll quit."

It hurt plenty during the 1957 season. Sometimes he played despite the pain. But at other times he told the manager: "I am sick. I cannot play."

Some baseball writers—and some players, too— began to call Roberto a whiner, a crybaby. Even worse, some said he was goldbricking.

Trainer Tony Bartirome works on Roberto's sore muscles.

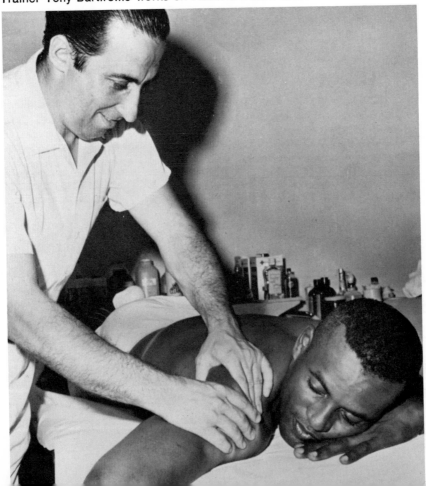

It was his worst year in the big leagues. His average was only .253. The team tied for last place with the Chicago Cubs. Manager Bragan was fired and a shrewd Irishman, Danny Murtaugh, took over.

That winter, Roberto trained with the Marine Reserve. Amazingly his back improved. He started the season in fine form.

The Pirates, on the other hand, were pretty bad. But Murtaugh coaxed them and bullied them. And slowly they climbed upward.

Roberto made a fast throw in one game and felt something snap in his arm. What was it? The doctors weren't sure. It hurt—but he played anyhow.

The Pirates came up from the cellar to second place, just eight games out of the top slot. It was the best season the team had had since 1944.

Roberto had played in 140 games in spite of his bad back and arm. His final average was .289. His fielding was improving, too.

The fans hungered for a pennant. People who hadn't been to a Pirates game in years came to cheer. But 1959 proved to be only a so-so year after all.

Roberto's injuries put him on the disabled list from May 25 until July 3. Other players were injured, too. Meanwhile, the Giants, Dodgers, and Braves were red-hot pennant contenders. The prize finally went to the Dodgers. The Pirates settled for fourth.

In a 1958 game against the Chicago Cubs, Roberto made a sensational back-handed catch of Bobby Thompsen's long drive. Team-mate Bill Virdon came to help, but was not needed.

They were still a good team. All they needed were the breaks. They finally got them in 1960.

Roberto still had pain, but he played in spite of it. At the end of May he was the league-leading hitter and the Pirates were in first place.

Roberto not only hit, but he also fielded like a star. He could leap out sideways to spear a drive, then fire the ball back almost before you realized he had caught it. He was very tired by September.

But the pennant was within reach.

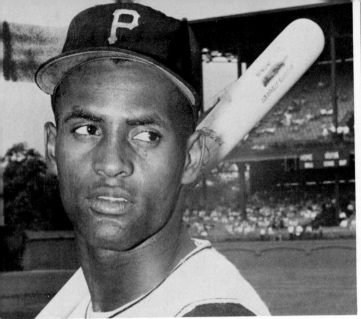

In the second 1960 World Series game, Roberto sent a "Texas league" single into short right center. Roger Maris is trying to scoop up the ball. Bobby Richardson *(left)* and Mickey Mantle *(background)* come in to assist. The Yankees won this game, 16-3.

On September 25, the Pirates played the Braves and lost, 4-2. But at the same time, the rival Cardinals lost to the Chicago Cubs. This gave the pennant to Pittsburgh for the first time since 1927.

In the World Series, they faced the awesome New York Yankees. The Yanks had fought in 10 of the last 13 World Series. They had won eight times. Nobody gave the lowly Pirates a chance to beat such a team.

Just the same, the Pirates went out and won the Series opener, 6-4. Fans yelled: "Beat 'em, Bucs!"

The next two games were disasters. The Yankees stomped the Pirates, 16-3 and 10-0. Sportscasters shook their heads. What did you expect?

Roberto spoke out against the jeering. "You just come back tomorrow! We will win!"

He was right. With better pitching by Vernon Law and ElRoy Face, the Pirates squeaked by with a 3-2 surprise victory. They won the next game, too, 5-2.

Roberto contributed a hit in each contest. But even though he was doing a great job, he sensed that other Pirates were getting more attention—especially the team's slugging captain, Dick Groat.

Back home in Pittsburgh, the Pirates lost to the Yankees by a humiliating 12-0. The Series was all tied up.

Roberto and Bill Virdon go for the ball in the fourth game of the 1960 World Series. Virdon batted in the winning runs and made a game-saving catch as the Pirates won, 3-2.

In the sixth World Series game, Roberto fields a six-inning triple to right field by Yankee third baseman Clete Boyer. The Pirates were crushed, 12-0.

The seventh game, played at home, would decide the championship.

The Pirates fought hard, but New York led by 7-4 in the bottom of the eighth inning. The fans held their breath with forlorn hope.

They saw their team explode. Dick Groat drove in a run. Clemente hit a single and another man came home. A home run by catcher Hal Smith put the Pirates ahead, 9-7. "Beat 'em, Bucs!" cried the crowd.

Then the Yanks tied the score. But young Bill Mazerowski of the Pirates had a cure for that. He walloped a home run.

The Pirates had won the World Series.

Roberto Clemente was glad. But something deep inside him made him avoid the locker-room party. Instead, he went off to be with the fans—his real friends.

Then he flew home to Puerto Rico.

Roberto hugs team-mate Hal Smith, whose home run allowed both him and Dick Groat to score. The Pirates won the final game 10-9 on October 13, 1960. They were World Series champions at last.

Roberto had batted .314 that year. He felt he had "carried" the team. But when the voting for Most Valuable Player was in, Dick Groat was the winner. Roberto Clemente came in eighth. It made him very bitter. His Latin pride was hurt.

All that saved him was the devotion of the fans. They began to make him their pet. When he came up to bat, they would yell: *"Arriba!"* Even though most of the crowd didn't know that the Spanish word meant something like, "Go get 'em," they still wanted to cheer Roberto in his own language.

He appreciated it—and played his heart out.

Dick Groat *(right),* the Pirates' slugging shortstop, was 1960's Most Valuable Player in the National League and batting titlist as well. This picture shows Groat congratulating Roberto Clemente on winning the 1961 batting title with a .351 average.

League President Warren Giles presents Roberto with a silver bat, symbol of the batting title.

On May 13, 1961, he got his 1,000th hit. Even though he continued to suffer aches and pains, he still managed to bat .351. He hit 23 home runs, batted in 89 runs, and led the league with 27 assists.

The two years that followed were only fair. His average was .312 in 1962 and .320 in 1963. The Pirates were in fourth place, then plummeted to the cellar.

Roberto Clemente was now recognized as a top baseball player. Unfortunately, he was also known for complaining of injuries. It was not his way to suffer in silence, as is the usual custom among ball players. When he hurt, he let people know it.

And some made fun of him.

His back and arm still ached in 1964. One day he went into a drug store in San Juan for some medicine. The druggist's beautiful daughter waited on him.

Roberto forgot the pain. He could think only of the lovely girl, Vera Zabala. All the rest of the year, he played magnificent baseball. Perhaps he was still thinking of Vera, wanting her to admire him.

He won his second batting title with an average of .339, the best in both leagues. And in November, he and Vera were married.

But the year that seemed so wonderful still had a month to go. In December, he was managing the San Juan baseball team—playing ball instead of resting. The fans had begged to see him play, and he could not bear to disappoint them.

But it would lead to another disaster.

He tore a ligament in the Puerto Rican All Star Game. Then he caught malaria. To top it off, he caught still another infection while working on his farm. Most men would have taken a year off.

But Roberto played. At first he was weak, but his power slowly returned. Limping and complaining to those who would listen, he nonetheless played in 152 games and won his third batting title. At .329, he was again king of both leagues. The Pirates, under a new manager, were in the number-three spot.

Roberto Clemente supervises work on his Puerto Rico farm.

On September 2, 1966, Roberto got his 2,000th major-league hit, a home run off the Chicago Cubs' Fergie Jenkins. Greeting him at the plate are Matty Alou *(18)* and Bob Veale *(39).*

Roberto was a top hitter with a high average. But he had never been much of a home-run slugger. This made many people say that he "lacked power."

When the 1966 season opened, Manager Harry Walker said: "Roberto, I want you to try to hit more homers. Try for more RBI's. We need them if we are to win the pennant."

"Sure," said Roberto—just as if it was easy.

The team missed the boat—just barely—and came in third that year. But Roberto Clemente did just as his coach asked. He hit 29 homers and batted in 119 runs—a career record. Even better, he became a team leader, inspiring the rest of the Pirates to do their best.

A triple-exposure photograph shows Roberto Clemente's swing.

Full of new confidence, Roberto dared to speak out about injustice in baseball.

"The Latin player doesn't get the recognition he deserves," he said. "Neither does the black player, unless he is spectacular, like Willie Mays. We have self-satisfaction. But when the season is over, nobody cares about us. We are outsiders. Foreigners. I am an American citizen, but some people act like I live in a jungle some place!"

But that was the year that people proved they cared about Roberto Clemente. He was voted Most Valuable Player in the National League by the Baseball Writers of America.

"I will treasure this all my life," he said.

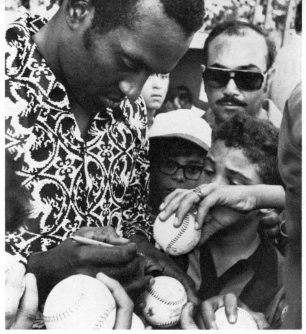
Puerto Rican youngsters clamor for Roberto to autograph their baseballs. His greatest dream was to build a Sports City for the children of his island.

Roberto Clemente was a national hero in Puerto Rico. But he remained unfamiliar to most stateside fans outside Pittsburgh. He was an "unsung super-star."

Did sportswriters avoid him because he talked so much about his injuries? Were they bored by his pride, that made him sensitive to jokes and horseplay? Or did they let him alone simply because he did not speak perfect English for the radio and television microphones?

Roberto did not know. But he kept on playing and winning. On May 15, 1967, he had his biggest game. He hit three home runs and a double, driving in seven runs.

But the Pirates lost to the Cincinnati Reds, 8-7. The team was only sixth in 1967. Roberto won his fourth batting title with an average of .357.

He was now making $100,000 a year, right up there with Hank Aaron and Willie Mays. He had a handsome home in Rio Piedras, a beautiful wife, and two little sons. He dreamed of building a Sports City for the children of Puerto Rico. Perhaps even more, he wanted to see his team on top again.

Danny Murtaugh came back to manage the Pirates in 1968. They came in sixth. In 1969 they managed to attain third. Injuries continued to plague Roberto. But he still came within a hair of winning the batting title. His average was .345. Pete Rose of Cincinnati had .348.

Manager Danny Murtagh checks on the state of Roberto's aches and pains.

Roberto was honored at "Roberto Clemente Night" in Shea Stadium, New York City, on September 25, 1971. Sharing the glory was his wife, Vera, and their three sons, Enrique, Roberto, Jr., and Luis.

Then came 1970. Roberto had a great year and so did the team. They were first in the Eastern Division, but lost the playoff to the Reds.

In 1971 the Pirates ran right over Cincinnati's "Big Red Machine" and took the pennant. Again, as in 1966, they were World Series underdogs as they faced the Baltimore Orioles.

Baltimore won the first two games at home. "It will be different when we get to Pittsburgh," Roberto said.

And it was. The Pirates took the third game, 5-1. Roberto had three hits in the fourth game, and the Pirates tied up the Series by winning, 4-3.

The fifth game, also played at Pittsburgh, was a 4-0 shutout by Pirate Nelson Briles. Then they went back to Baltimore—and nobody gave them a chance.

In a 10-inning heart-stopper, Baltimore won the sixth game, 3-2. The last game was scoreless until the fourth inning. Then Roberto hit a home run.

Visions of 1960 danced before the Pittsburgh fans. Could their team pull off a second World Series upset? The Pirates brought another man home in the eighth inning. Then the Orioles scored. But at the end, the Pirates were the victors, 2-1.

Everyone agreed Roberto was the hero of the Series. He had batted .414, playing in all seven games. He had hammered two home runs and 12 hits, with 4 RBI's.

His comment after the Series has been misunderstood. He said, "For me, I am the best." It was an old Spanish saying meaning, "I do the best I can."

Roberto homers in the fourth inning of the seventh World Series game, October 17, 1971.

Now there was glory for Roberto on the mainland as well as in his home island. He was called the best all-around player in baseball. On September 30, 1972, he achieved another goal: he got his 3,000th hit.

At home in Puerto Rico, he was full of plans for the Sports City for children. Then, in December, there was a terrible earthquake in Managua, Nicaragua.

Roberto wanted to help. He collected supplies, medicine, and money. He wanted to fly them to Nicaragua himself to make sure that they reached the poor who needed them most.

Roberto Clemente became the eleventh man to reach the 3,000-hit mark by slamming a double in a game against the Mets at Pittsburgh.

Baseball Commissioner Bowie Kuhn announces that Roberto Clemente has been elected to Baseball's Hall of Fame by a landslide vote. Mrs. Clemente is at his side.

The prop-driven airplane he hired was old. It had engine trouble before it took off, but then seemed to be all right. On December 31, 1972, Roberto Clemente and four others took off for Nicaragua.

Not long after, the old airplane crashed into the sea. Rescuers searched in vain for Roberto's body.

The Governor-elect of Puerto Rico, Rafael Hernandez Colon, said of him:

"Roberto died serving his fellow man. Our youth lose an idol. Our people lose one of their glories."

46

Roberto Clemente of the Pittsburgh Pirates, holding a bat that symbolized his position as the club's all-time RBI leader.

ROBERTO WALKER CLEMENTE

He was born August 18, 1934, at Carolina, Puerto Rico, and graduated from Julio Coronado Bezcarrondo High School. In 1952, while he was still in high school, he played for the Santurce Crabbers of the Puerto Rican Winter League. Throughout much of his big-league career, he played part-time in the Winter League. From 1952-1956 he was with Santurce. He played for Caguas 1957-1960 and for San Juan 1960-1962, 1963-1966, and 1969-1971.

In 1954 he played for the Montreal Royals of the AAA International League, a Dodgers farm club. He was drafted by Pittsburgh according to the regulation in force that year (and only that year).

He played for the Pittsburgh Pirates from 1955 through 1972. On November 14, 1964, he married Vera Zabala. The couple had three sons.

Roberto Clemente died December 31, 1972, off San Juan in an airplane crash at sea. The Sports City he dreamed of building will carry his name.

ROBERTO CLEMENTE STATISTICS

Year	Club	G	AB	H	2B	3B	HR	RBI	BA
1954	Montreal	87	148	38	5	3	2	12	.257
1955	Pittsburgh	124	474	121	23	11	5	47	.255
1956	Pittsburgh	147	543	169	30	7	7	60	.311
1957	Pittsburgh	111	451	114	17	7	4	30	.253
1958	Pittsburgh	140	519	150	24	10	6	50	.289
1959	Pittsburgh	105	432	128	17	7	4	50	.296
1960	Pittsburgh	144	570	179	22	6	16	94	.314
1961	Pittsburgh	146	572	201	30	10	23	89	.351**
1962	Pittsburgh	144	538	168	28	9	10	74	.312
1963	Pittsburgh	152	600	192	23	8	17	76	.320
1964	Pittsburgh	155	622	211*	40	7	12	87	.339**
1965	Pittsburgh	152	589	194	21	14	10	65	.329**
1966	Pittsburgh	154	638	202	31	11	29	119	.317
1967	Pittsburgh	147	585	209**	26	10	23	110	.357**
1968	Pittsburgh	132	502	146	18	12	18	57	.291
1969	Pittsburgh	138	507	175	20	12**	19	91	.345
1970	Pittsburgh	108	412	145	22	10	14	60	.352
1971	Pittsburgh	132	522	178	29	8	13	86	.341
1972	Pittsburgh	102	378	118	19	7	10	60	.312
	M.L. TOTALS	2433	9454	3000	440	166	240	1305	.317

* Tied League Leader
** League Leader

Most Valuable Player: 1966
Most Valuable Player, World Series: 1971
Gold Glove Award (fielding): 1961, 1962, 1963, 1964, 1965, 1966, 1967, 1968, 1969, 1970, 1971, 1972

First Latin player elected to Baseball's Hall of Fame, March 10, 1973